# My Family and Me

## A MEMORY SCRAPBOOK
## FOR KIDS

written by
**JANE DRAKE and ANN LOVE**

illustrated by
**SCOT RITCHIE**

**KIDS CAN PRESS**

# My Family and Me

My name is _____ _____ _____.
                    *(first)*                *(middle)*          *(last)*

My family calls me _____, because

_____.

I was born on _____ _____, _____,
                    *(month)*              *(day)*    *(year)*

and so I am _____ years old.

I was born in _____, _____.
                 *(city or town)*          *(country)*

In my family, I am the

☐ oldest child

☐ youngest child

☐ only child

☐ _____

My mother's name is _____ _____ _____ .
　　　　　　　　　　　　　　*(first)*　　　　　　*(middle)*　　　　*(last)*

She was born in _____ , _____ , on
　　　　　　　　　*(city or town)*　　　　*(country)*

_____ _____ , _____ .
*(month)*　　　　　　　*(day)*　　　　　*(year)*

My father's name is _____ _____ _____ .
　　　　　　　　　　　　　*(first)*　　　　　　*(middle)*　　　　*(last)*

He was born in _____ , _____ , on
　　　　　　　　*(city or town)*　　　　*(country)*

_____ _____ , _____ .
*(month)*　　　　　　　*(day)*　　　　　*(year)*

I have _____ brothers/stepbrothers and _____ sisters/stepsisters.
　　　　　*(circle one or both)*　　　　　　　　　　　*(circle one or both)*

Their names are

_____ , _____ , _____ , _____ .

# The Way It Is

In our family, we do things our own way.

First thing in the morning we
- [ ] fight for the bathroom
- [ ] gobble up our breakfasts
- [ ] check the sports scores
- [ ] _____

Before bed we always
- [ ] bring in the cat
- [ ] drink hot chocolate
- [ ] set our alarm clocks
- [ ] _____

On the weekends we look forward to
- [ ] sleeping late
- [ ] going for a run together
- [ ] big breakfasts
- [ ] _____

As a special treat, we
- [ ] order in our favorite food
- [ ] go hiking
- [ ] go out for ice cream
- [ ] _____

Every day, my mother ⬜ goes to work

⬜ picks me up from school

⬜ helps me with my homework

⬜ _____

Every day, my father ⬜ goes to work

⬜ cooks dinner

⬜ reads to me

⬜ _____

Every day, I have to

⬜ straighten my room

⬜ set the table

⬜ brush the dog's teeth

⬜ _____

When I get a little older, I'll be allowed to

⬜ ride my bike to the store

⬜ go to a movie with a friend

⬜ take the bus by myself

⬜ use the lawn mower

⬜ _____

# My Grandparents

On my mother's side, my grandmother's name is _____.

I call her _____.

She was born on _____, in _____, _____.
                             *(date)*                             *(city or town)*            *(country)*

On my mother's side, my grandfather's name is _____.

I call him _____.

He was born on _____, in _____, _____.
                             *(date)*                             *(city or town)*            *(country)*

Here is a picture of

my grandparents.

A friend of my family who is like a grandparent to me is

_____.

On my father's side, my grandmother's name is _____.

I call her _____.

She was born on _____, in _____, _____.
                    *(date)*                *(city or town)*      *(country)*

On my father's side, my grandfather's name is _____.

I call him _____.

He was born on _____, in _____, _____.
                   *(date)*                *(city or town)*      *(country)*

Here is a picture of

my grandparents.

My mother/father got married again, so I have new grandparents.
   *(circle one or both)*

Their names are _____ and _____.

# Aunts, Uncles and More!

I have aunts and uncles who are

☐ related to my mother

☐ related to my father

☐ not really related at all

☐ _____

Here are some of my aunts and uncles:

My mother's sisters and brothers          My father's sisters and brothers

_____                    _____

_____                    _____

_____                    _____

We have close family friends that I call

☐ Aunt _____          ☐ _____

☐ Uncle _____         ☐ _____

I'm lucky that I have  ☐ an aunt about the same age as me to play with.

☐ an uncle

☐ a cousin

☐ _____

Counting cousins, I have

☐ dozens of cousins

☐ a few cousins

☐ no cousins at all

☐ _____

My first cousins are my aunts' and uncles' children. These are the first cousins I know best:

_____  _____  _____  _____

My mother and father have cousins, and their children are my second cousins.

My second cousins

☐ are a lot older than I am

☐ live far away

☐ send me e-mail

☐ _____

 # Surrounded by Family

Some members of my family live with me and some don't, but they're all important to me.

These are the family members I see all the time:

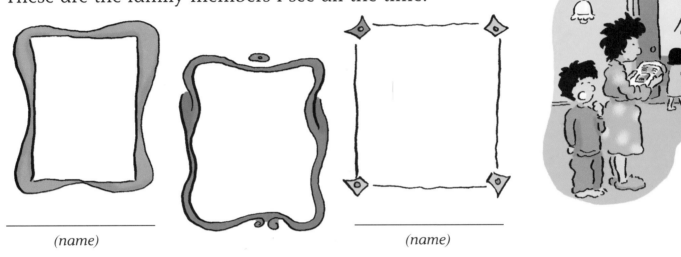

*(name)*

*(name)*

*(name)*

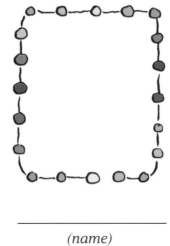

*(name)*

*(name)*

*(name)*

These are the family members I see a few times a year:

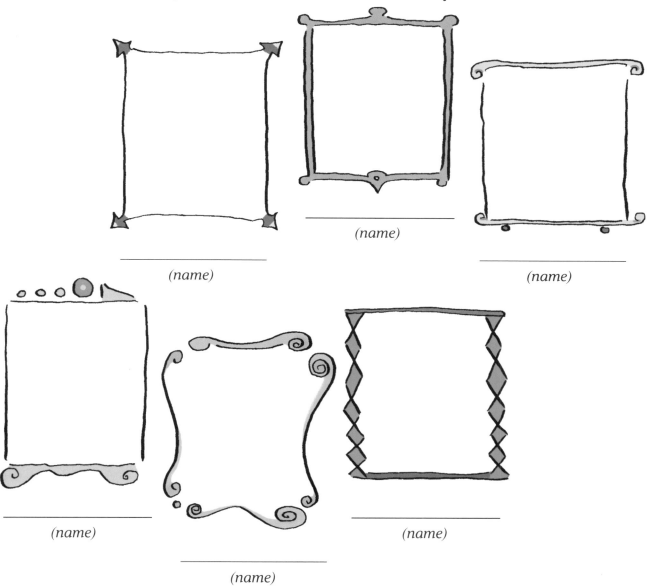

*(name)*

*(name)*

*(name)*

*(name)*

*(name)*

*(name)*

Family members I hardly ever see are _____,

_____, _____, _____.

# Family Characters

When I count all the people in my family, I have _____ relatives.
Many of them are special and interesting to me.

_____ always makes me laugh out loud,
*(relative's name)*

especially when _____.

The most stubborn person in my family is _____,
*(relative's name)*

especially when _____.

_____ is the bossiest member of the family,
*(relative's name)*

especially when _____.

People say I'm just like _____ when I _____.
*(relative's name)*

When we all get together, we are

☐ always laughing

☐ quiet as mice

☐ a wild and crazy bunch

☐ _____

If I used one word to describe my family, I would say

we are _____.

Of all my relatives, I like to spend the most time with _____.

We like to _____ together.

Here is a picture of the two of us.

# Family Features

Am I a lot like other people in my family or just like myself?

In our family, most people have                    I have

☐              dark hair                    ☐

☐              fair hair                    ☐

☐              curly hair                   ☐

☐              straight hair                ☐

☐         _____ hair                 ☐

☐              brown eyes                   ☐

☐              blue eyes                    ☐

☐              hazel eyes                   ☐

☐         _____ eyes                 ☐

Most of my relatives are    ☐ tall
                            ☐ short
                            ☐ in between

I am _____.

Some people in my family can

- [ ] cross their eyes
- [ ] roll their tongues
- [ ] sit cross-legged
- [ ] wiggle their ears
- [ ] do the splits
- [ ] _____

I'm one of the people in my family who can _____.

Of all the people in my family, _____ is the tallest.

_____ is the shortest.

_____ has the most freckles.

_____ has the biggest feet.

_____ has the knobbiest knees.

_____ has the bushiest eyebrows.

# Family Treasures

My family keeps these old treasures *(circle the picture)*:

My mother's favorite family treasure is _____

because _____.

My father's favorite family treasure is _____

because _____.

My family's weirdest keepsake is _____.

Here's the story behind it:

_____

_____

_____

Whenever I look at _____ I think of my

grandfather/grandmother.
*(circle one or both)*

The best gift I ever got from someone in my family is _____

from _____ .
    *(relative's name)*

_____ says that he/she will always keep
*(relative's name)*               *(circle one)*

the _____ from me.

Here is a picture of something that is special just to me:

I will treasure it forever because _____

_____ .

# Family Pastimes

My family enjoys tons of activities — some together, some solo.

In my family, we play

☐ friendly card games          ☐ serious chess matches

☐ noisy video games           ☐ _____

I learned to play the game of _____ from _____.

*(relative's name)*

My family is known for

☐ baking yummy cookies

☐ growing huge pumpkins

☐ building crazy sandcastles

☐ _____

I want to learn how to make _____ from _____.

*(relative's name)*

My family's favorite activity is

☐ ice hockey

☐ soccer

☐ yoga

☐ _____

There are lots of talented people in my family.

_____ is the best singer.

_____ is the best musician.

_____ is the best dancer.

_____ is the best artist.

_____ is the best comedian.

I am the only one in my family who is talented at _____.

People in my family like collecting

▢ stamps

▢ sports cards

▢ funny-shaped rocks

▢ _____

The weirdest collection in our family is the _____

collection that _____ owns.
        (relative's name)

I have a good collection of _____.

19

 # Our Family Celebrations

Whenever my family gets together, in a big group or small, we have fun at our parties.

Every year we celebrate

- ☐ New Year
- ☐ Hanukkah
- ☐ Thanksgiving
- ☐ Passover
- ☐ Eid
- ☐ _____
- ☐ Christmas
- ☐ Kwanzaa

Sometimes we celebrate

- ☐ the birth of a baby
- ☐ confirmations
- ☐ Bar/Bat Mitzvahs
- ☐ graduations
- ☐ weddings
- ☐ _____

My favorite kind of family celebration is _____, because

_____ .

At family parties, I like extra helpings of _____,
(name of food)

made by _____.
(name of relative)

One decoration we use each _____ is _____.
(name of celebration)

The funniest thing that ever happened at a family

celebration was _____

_____.

I'll never forget the time when _____ said,
(relative's name)

" _____."

The biggest mess we ever had at a family party was

_____.

# Family Travels

The first member of my family to come to this part of the country was

_____, on _____.
(relative's name)                            (date)

Here is what I know about that journey:

_____

_____

_____

Since I was born, my family has

moved _____ times.

The relatives who live farthest away from me are _____.

They live in _____.

The relatives who live closest to me are _____.

They live in _____.

A place my family likes to visit on vacation is _____.

The best place we've ever been is _____.

Here is a picture of us there:

My special memory from there is _____
_____.

Someday my family would like to travel to _____

because _____.

# Telling Family Tales

Each time these family stories are told, they get a little better.

The best story the family tells about me is _____

_____

_____

_____.

I like it best when _____ tells this story
(relative's name)

because _____.

The best pet story my family tells is _____

_____

_____

_____.

I like it best when _____ tells this story
(relative's name)

because _____.

The scariest story my family tells is _____

_____

_____

_____.

The best family joke goes like this:

_____

_____

_____

_____

One family story I will always remember and tell is _____

_____

_____

_____.

# The Olden Days

We remember our ancestors from

☐ family stories and sayings      ☐ old photographs

☐ newspaper clippings      ☐ _____

These are my great-grandparents (my grandparents' parents) on

my mother's side:

_____, _____ — _____
(name)               (born)          (died)

_____, _____ — _____
(name)               (born)          (died)

_____, _____ — _____
(name)               (born)          (died)

_____, _____ — _____
(name)               (born)          (died)

The earliest relative we know about on my mother's side is _____,

who lived in _____ about the year _____.
                 (place)

If I could travel back in time, one of my mother's ancestors I'd like

to meet is _____.

I would ask him/her about _____.
          (circle one)

These are my great-grandparents (my grandparents' parents) on
my father's side:

_____, _____ — _____
(name)                        (born)            (died)

_____, _____ — _____
(name)                        (born)            (died)

_____, _____ — _____
(name)                        (born)            (died)

_____, _____ — _____
(name)                        (born)            (died)

The earliest relative we know about on my father's side is _____,

who lived in _____ about the year _____.
                    (place)

If I could travel back in time, one of my father's ancestors I'd like

to meet is _____.

I would ask him/her about _____.
                (circle one)

# Once Upon a Time

Stories about my ancestors make me feel like I know them.

This is the story I like to hear over and over again about my family in olden times:

_____

_____

_____

_____

The saddest story about one of my ancestors goes like this:

_____

_____

_____

_____

 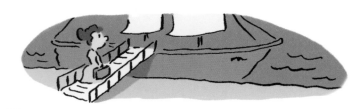

The funniest story about one of my ancestors always makes me laugh, and here it is:

_____

_____

_____

_____

The most dangerous time my ancestors lived through was

_____

_____

_____

_____.

One ancestor I want to be like is _____

because _____.

# My Family Tree

_____
Great-grandfather
(Grandfather's father)

_____
Great-grandfather
(Grandmother's father)

_____
Great-grandmother
(Grandfather's mother)

_____
Great-grandmother
(Grandmother's mother)

_____
Grandfather
(Father's father)

_____
Grandmother
(Father's mother)

_____
Father

More of Father's Family:

_____

_____

_____

_____

_____

_____

_____
Me

_____

_____

_____

_____

Brothers/Sisters

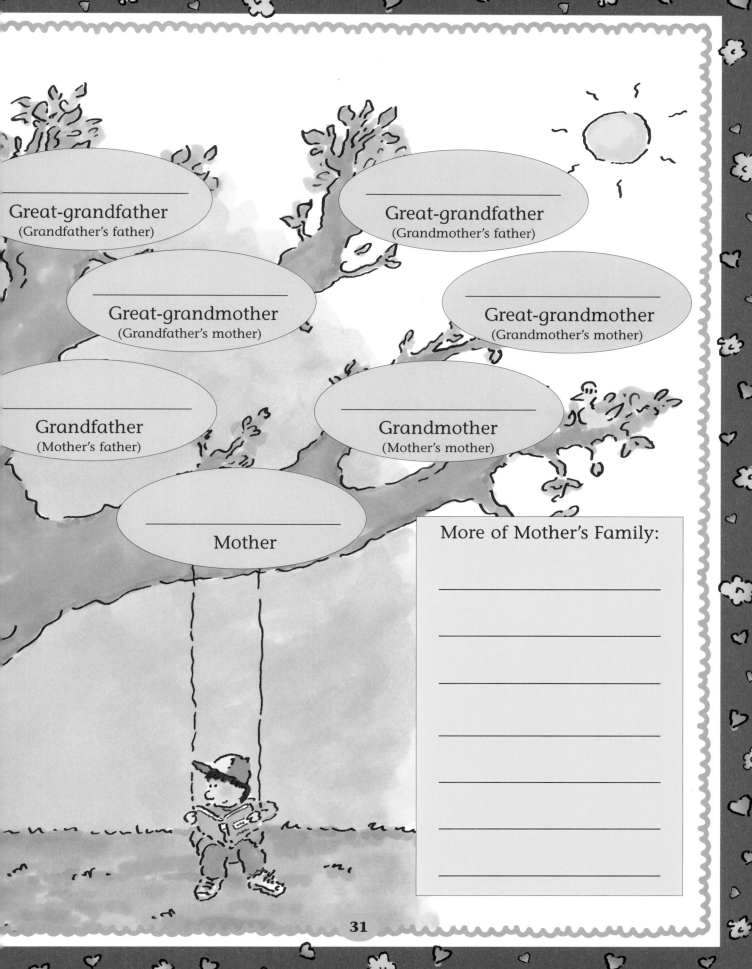

_____
Great-grandfather
(Grandfather's father)

_____
Great-grandfather
(Grandmother's father)

_____
Great-grandmother
(Grandfather's mother)

_____
Great-grandmother
(Grandmother's mother)

_____
Grandfather
(Mother's father)

_____
Grandmother
(Mother's mother)

_____
Mother

More of Mother's Family:

_____

_____

_____

_____

_____

_____

_____

31

To Aunt Doreen, keeper of our family history — J.D. and A.L.

To Aunt June for keeping the records — S.R.

Text © 2002 Jane Drake and Ann Love
Illustrations © 2002 Scot Ritchie

Published in Canada by
Kids Can Press Ltd.
29 Birch Avenue
Toronto, ON  M4V 1E2

Published in the U.S. by
Kids Can Press Ltd.
2250 Military Road
Tonawanda, NY  14150

www.kidscanpress.com

Edited by Kat Mototsune
Designed by Stacie Bowes

Printed in Hong Kong by Wing King Tong Co. Ltd.

CM 02  0 9 8 7 6 5 4 3 2 1

ISBN 1-55337-002-3

Kids Can Press is a Nelvana company